(hello!!)

Here's *Hoshin Engi* volume 2. Compared to volume 1, Supushan seems to have gained weight. That's worrisome. I may draw a story called "Supushan Goes on a Diet." Or I may not.

Ryu Fujisaki

Ryu Fujisaki's *Worlds* came in second place for the prestigious 40th Tezuka Award. His *Psycho +*, *Wāqwāq* and *Hoshin Engi* have all run in *Weekly Shonen Jump* magazine, and *Hoshin Engi* anime is available on DVD in Japan and North America. A lover of science fiction, literature and history, Fujisaki has made *Hoshin Engi* a mix of genres that truly showcases his amazing art and imagination.

HOSHIN ENGI VOL. 2
The SHONEN JUMP Manga Edition

STORY AND ART BY RYU FUJISAKI
Based on the novel *Hoshin Engi*, translated by Tsutomu Ano, published by Kodansha Bunko

Translation & English Adaptation/Tomo Kimura
Touch-up Art & Lettering/Rina Mapa
Design/Sean Lee
Editor/Joel Enos

Editor in Chief, Books/Alvin Lu
Editor in Chief, Magazines/Marc Weidenbaum
VP of Publishing Licensing/Rika Inouye
VP of Sales/Gonzalo Ferreyra
Sr. VP of Marketing/Liza Coppola
Publisher/Hyoe Narita

Printed in the U.S.A.

Published by VIZ Media, LLC
P.O. Box 77010
San Francisco, CA 94107

SHONEN JUMP Manga Edition
10 9 8 7 6 5 4 3 2 1
First printing, August 2007

HOSHIN ENGI™

封神演義

VOL. 2
CHANGES

STORY AND ART BY
RYU FUJISAKI

The Story Thus Far

Ancient China. Three thousand years ago. The Yin Dynasty Era.

King Chu was a good king, a master in the arts of pen and sword. But when he married the beautiful ***Dakki***, he changed. For Dakki was a Sennyo with a wicked heart who turned poor King Chu into her political puppet. Dakki and her comrades took control of the dynasty and now live in luxury at the people's expense.

To save the human world, the ***Hoshin Project*** was created. The project's mission is to seal evil Sennin and Doshi into the Shinkai, a nebulous netherworld prison. The wise ***Genshi Tenson*** chose the Doshi ***Taikobo*** to head the project.

Taikobo targeted Dakki, planning to defeat her, causing her minions to scatter and thus be swiftly rounded up. But Dakki is not easily conquered, and the price for defying Dakki is death!

THE CHARACTERS

A POWERFUL DOSHI WITH A STRANGE SENSE OF HUMOR AND UNKNOWN LOYALTIES.

SHINKOHYO

KOKUTENKO

SHINKOHYO'S REIJU.

DAKKI

AN EVIL SENNIN HAS POSSESSED THE BODY OF THE QUEEN. HER BEAUTY BELIES HER EVIL.

KING CHU

THE FORMER GOOD EMPEROR OF THE YIN DYNASTY IS NOW THE PUPPET OF HIS QUEEN, DAKKI.

SUPUSHAN

TAIKOBO'S FAITHFUL REIJU.

TAIKOBO (AKA KYOSHIGA)

A DOSHI WHO'D RATHER JUST HANG OUT THAN BE THE HEAD OF THE HOSHIN PROJECT!

VOL. 2
CHANGES

CONTENTS

Chapter 8

THE END OF THE BEGINNING

WAAAAAAAH!
SHOVE

GIGGLE

THE NEXT 40, COME FORWARD!
HURRY UP!

BY THE WAY, TAIKOBO IS TODAY'S MAIN ATTRACTION. ♡
I'LL BURN HIS ARMS AND LEGS WITH THE HORAKU, AND THEN DROP HIM INTO THE TAIBON. A SPECIAL COURSE.♡

EMPRESS!

BOW

IF YOU CONTINUE TO COMMIT SUCH ACTS OF CRUELTY, YOU WILL LOSE THE LOVE OF THE PEOPLE.

PLEASE STOP!

YOU GO TOO FAR, BUSEIO. ♡

HAVE YOU FORGOTTEN THAT THE FATE OF YOUR SISTER IS IN MY HANDS?

CLENCH
Clench
!!
YANK
HEY, DON'T MOVE!

EVERY-BODY...
...RUN! RUN AWAY!

WHAT'RE YOU SAYING?!

WHOSE FAULT IS THIS?!

IT'S ALL BECAUSE OF YOU!

YOU DON'T HAVE ANY POWER AT ALL!

YOU DROP INTO THE TAIBON ONE BY ONE!

YOU STINK!

OUCH!

KICK

HEY HEY, KEEP QUIET!

DO

OH ...

CEASE TO SPEAK!

YOU ...

... NOOOOO!

EVERY-ONE! SLAVES OR NO, WE MUST FIGHT!

WE CAN'T DIE LIKE THIS!

BAM

OOOH.

NOW'S MY CHANCE!

FWOOO

HOW BARBARIC! SUPU, LET'S FLY UP. ♡

AHHHHHH

BAM

BAM

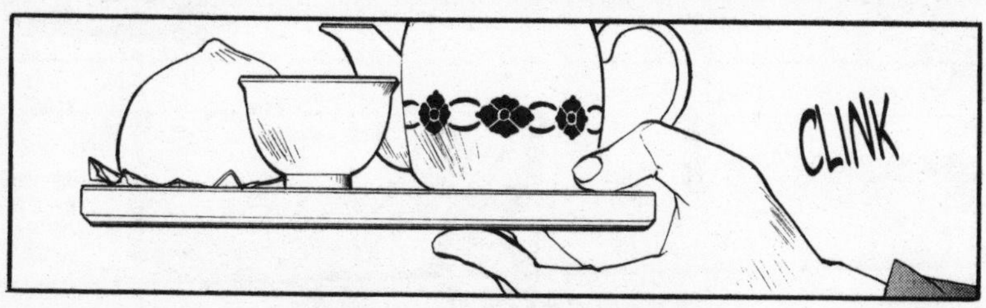
CLINK

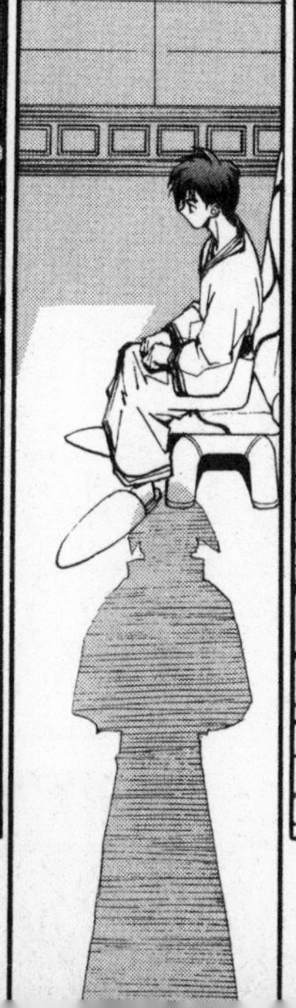

EH.
KA
WHAM

YOU'RE AWAKE.

YOU WANNA EAT SOME-THING?

YOUR RIBS ARE BROKEN. AMONG OTHER THINGS.

STAY HERE WHILE YOU RECU-PERATE.

WE ARE COMPLETELY HIDDEN HERE.

NOT EVEN THE EMPRESS CAN FIND US HERE.

...

Scratch

THE QIANGS WERE ALL KILLED...

...BY THE EMPRESS' MINIONS.

UM... WELL ...

I PUT YOUR CLOTHES IN THE SNAKE PIT.

YOU'RE SUPPOSED TO BE DEAD.

...

WHY DID YOU SAVE ME?

I'VE MADE A FATAL MISTAKE.
TAIKOBO!
AS SOON AS I MET YOU, I FELT...
...THAT YOU COULD DO SOME-THING.
I DIDN'T JUST SAVE YOUR LIFE! I LET YOU LIVE BECAUSE THE WORLD NEEDS YOU!
LIVE!
I WILL MAKE SURE OF YOUR SURVIVAL!

...
I MUST DO WHAT I MUST.

I had this made to look like the clothes you wore. Wear them if you want to. And I put that scroll on the shelf.

POUR

SPLOSH

I HAVE LOST ...

...MANY MANY THINGS ...

POUR

YOU DISAPPOINT ME.

GRIN

WHY'RE YOU SMILING?
You give me the creeps.

KOKU-TENKO!
SHUFFLE

SLAM

SPLASH

I TOOK HIM AWAY WHILE DAKKI WAS IN THE LADIES' ROOM.
I REMOVED THE POISON FROM HIM TOO.
SHK

NOW YOU OWE ME ONE.
TOSS

SLAP

YOU TOOK THE PAOPE BACK. THAT MEANS YOU HAVEN'T GIVEN UP.
GOOD SHOW.
I'M GLAD.

BUT YOU MUST AMUSE ME MUCH MORE.
BEFORE I WRITE OFF YOUR DEBT.

DAKKI WON THIS TIME WITHOUT LIFTING A PRETTY FINGER.
FLOAT
I WILL NOT ALLOW THAT TO HAPPEN AGAIN.
SHEESH...
...SHIN-KOHYO, YOU'RE SO WHIMSICAL.

BOING

UNH...

MASTER?

UM... WHERE ARE WE?

IT'S ABOUT TIME YOU WOKE UP!
WE'RE LEAVING!

I THOUGHT OVER THINGS WHILE YOU WERE ASLEEP, SUPU.
I REALIZE THAT I CAN'T DEFEAT DAKKI ALONE.
SO I SHALL GO MAKE ALLIES WHO CAN FIGHT AGAINST HER!
ALLIES?
YES.

LET'S MAKE A HUGE ALLY!

TAIKOBO EVENTUALLY MAKES SEIKI, A VAST REGION, HIS ALLY.

封神演義

Chapter 9

NATAKU!!

TAIKO-BO
...
HUNH

...SINCE YOU LEFT, THE EMPRESS DAKKI IS EVEN MORE BRUTAL.

SHE USES THE HORAKU TO BURN THOSE SHE DOES NOT FAVOR. AND SHE USES THE TAIBON WITHOUT MERCY.
THE PEOPLE OF CHOKA ARE DESPERATE TO ACHIEVE FAVOR WITH THE EMPRESS.

MONSTER!

THAT SIGHT SHOWED ME THE REALITY OF THE FALL OF YIN.

THE EMPRESS WAS DEVOURING THOSE SHE SHOVED INTO THE TAIBON...
SLURP
SLURP

DAKKI IS TRULY A MONSTER!

WE CAN'T GO ON LIKE THIS! WE HAVE TO DO SOMETHING...
WE MUST ELIMINATE HER AS SOON AS POSSIBLE!

MASTER-RRRRRR!

A PEACH! I FOUND SOME PEACHES!
THANK YOU, SUPU!

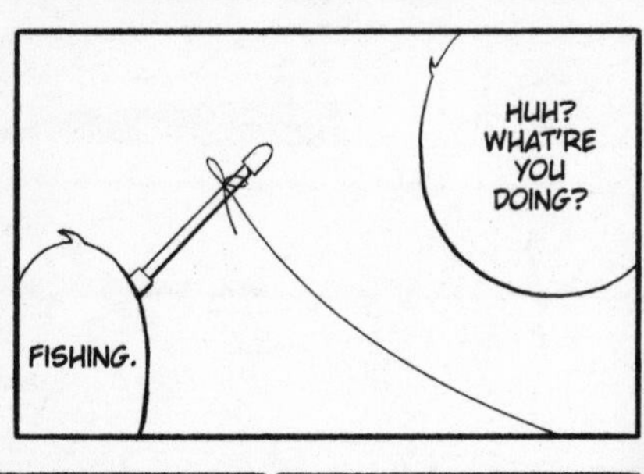
HUH? WHAT'RE YOU DOING?
FISHING.

FISHING?
A DOSHI SHOULDN'T EAT FISH.
I KNOW! I WON'T EAT IT! IT'S JUST A HOBBY.
CHOMP
THIS IS A GREAT PLACE TO RELAX.
SEE, LOOK AT THE SHAPE OF THE HOOK.
PLOOSH
THAT'S USELESS...

AND YOU THINK THAT WE DESERVE TO RELAX?
DON'T KNOW ...

DAKKI'S SO POWERFUL, I CAN'T REALLY DEFEAT HER YET.
GLAZE

SO *WE* MAKE STRONG ALLIES AS WELL!
YOU JUST MENTIONED IT THE OTHER DAY! TAIKOBO... DO YOU REALLY INTEND TO DO YOUR WORK?!

WHAT DO YOU THINK? BUT IF WE STAY HERE, WE MAY FISH A BIG ONE.
GLAZE

ZOMBI
HE'S BEEN WORKING TOO HARD.

CLICK

SHOOOM

MY SON'S GOING TO KILL ME!

H...
DASH
What, what?
...HELP MEEEE!

...
HUH?

SSSSSHHHH

SHHOOM

HE'S
MY
SON...
FWOOM

SCREECH

...NATAKU, A HUMAN PAOPE!
NATAKU?! I'VE HEARD THAT NAME SOMEWHERE.
A HUMAN PAOPE... SOMEONE RELATED TO THE SENNIN WORLD...
FWOOM
GIN
HE'S WEARING THREE PAOPE, YET HE LOOKS UNFAZED ...
WHO IS HE?!

...THE PAOPE KENKONKEN!

BO

HUH?

?!

Hmm?

WHY'RE YOU HERE?

Sob sob

DON'T LEAVE ME BEHIND!

YOU...

...

WHAT HAPPENED, STRANGER?

NO... NOTHING.

OH, STRANGER! NATAKU IS AFTER US!
SSSSHHHH

THOSE ARE FUKARIN, A FLYING PAOPE! ONLY ONE PAIR EXISTS IN THE SENNIN WORLD!

HE *IS* PERSISTENT. WHAT DID YOU DO TO MAKE HIM SO ANGRY?
I'LL TELL YOU LATER! PLEASE RUN AWAY NOW!

ALL RIGHT. SUPUSHAN, FLY INTO THE FOREST!
GRRR
ROGER!
SUPU-SHAN?

SHOOM

...

SSSSSH

FLI
CK

KABAMM

BOOM

FLICK

SPLINTER

SSSHHH
SSSSSHHH

...

COUGH COUGH
SHOOM
!
THE DUST CLOUD ...

SSSSS
HHH
NOOOOO, HE'S HERE!

WHAT THE...?! DOES HE MEAN TO KILL YOU?!
HE DOES!

HE HAS NO HEART, NO HUMAN FEELINGS!
HE'S MERCILESS!
TIME FOR ACTIONS, NOT REDUNDANT WORDS, MY FRIEND!

CLING
I WON'T LET GO! I WON'T LET GO!
WAAH! WHAT ARE YOU DOING ?!

PLEASE HELP ME!
ALL RIGHT, ALL RIGHT! LET GO!

THIS DOESN'T CONCERN ME!
AHHHHH
KICK
Y... YOU'RE BEING CRUEL.

AND?
SSSSSHHHH
WHAT'S THE STORY?

I CAN FEEL SENKI FROM YOU TOO.
WHO ARE YOU?
YOU ARE INDEED THE FIRST DISCIPLE OF GENSHI TENSON-SAMA, TAIKOBO.
I KNEW IT WAS YOU! YOU RIDE THE WHITE REIJU SUPUSHAN.

MY NAME IS SEI LI.
I HAVE TRAINED UNDER DOYAKU SHINJIN OF THE KONGRONG MOUNTAINS IN THE SENNIN WORLD.

BY THE WAY, SEI LI AND NATAKU APPEAR IN THE FAMOUS BOOK SAIYUKI (JOURNEY TO THE WEST) BY CHENG'EN WU, WRITTEN IN THE LATE 1500S.
IT MAY BE FUN TO CHECK THAT STORY OUT.

OH MASTER, LOOK!
HE'S A LITTLE SLOWER THAN I AM!

A REIJU IS FASTER THAN A PAOPE!
BEAMING IN PRIDE

AND WHO IS THAT CHILD?
YOU WEREN'T LISTENING.

(Senrigan allows Supushan to see anywhere, up to any distance so he can always keep Taikobo well informed.)

NATAKU...
...IS AN ARTIFICIAL HUMAN CREATED BY THE SENNIN WORLD.
?!
REIJU, SAID TO BE THE BEST PAOPE CREATED BY SENNIN...
BY EMBEDDING IT IN A HUMAN FEMALE, IT CAN CREATE A BORN SENNIN...
THAT'S WHAT NATAKU IS.
SCREECH
...
SHOOOM

THE TECHNOLOGY OF THE SENNIN WORLD HAS REACHED A POINT WHERE THEY CAN CREATE HUMANS.

AND THAT REIJU WAS EMBEDDED IN MY WIFE.

CLICK

BUT THE RESULT WAS...

...A COLD-HEARTED, RUTHLESS HUMAN WITHOUT A HEART.

封神演義

Chapter 10

THE BIRTH OF NATAKU

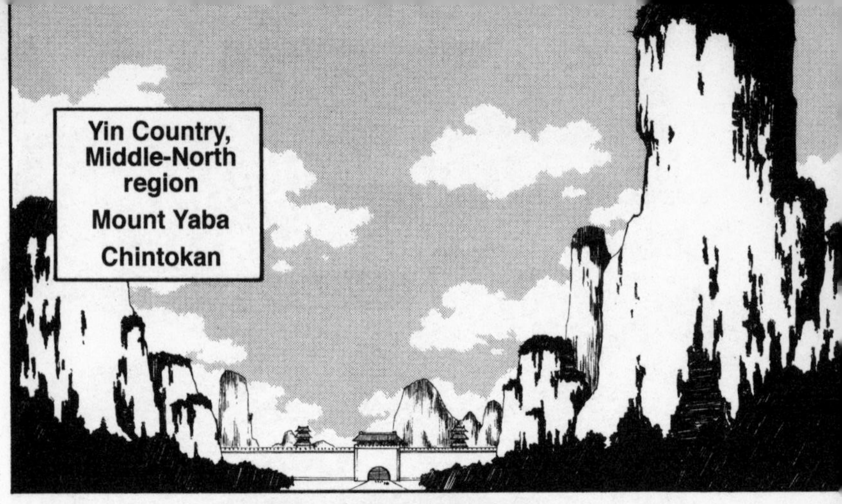
Yin Country, Middle-North region
Mount Yaba
Chintokan

MY DEAR!
Oh it's Sei Li!
You're alive!
WELCOME HOME!

OH INSHI! I WAS ALMOST KILLED BY NATAKU!
WHAP
OH DEAR! NATAKU CAN'T BE SERIOUS!

OH? WHO ARE THESE PEOPLE?

TAIKOBO AND SUPUSHAN.
THEY JUST SAVED ME, AND WILL PROTECT ME FROM NOW ON. THEY'RE GOOD!
Hey!

Sign says Chinto Kan ↓ ↖Checkpoint: a place that inspects people passing through, built at strategically important spots.

HE'S A COLD-HEARTED, RUTHLESS, CRUEL, AND MERCILESS MONSTER! HE'S EVIL!
WATCH YOUR MOUTH. HE'S JUST A TOUGH SON!
AND NATAKU ...
NATAKU ?!

BUT...I WAS A FAILURE...AND I COULDN'T GET A PAOPE...
BLUSH

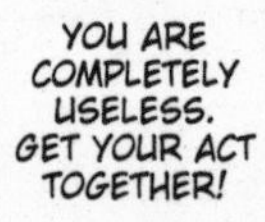
YOU ARE COMPLETELY USELESS. GET YOUR ACT TOGETHER!

Stare
Ha

SIGH
ENOUGH! TELL ME ABOUT NATAKU!

STAB
IF YOU'VE TRAINED IN THE SENNIN WORLD, YOU SHOULD BE ABLE TO DEAL WITH NATAKU!

PLEASE HELP US. WE'RE IN SUCH TROUBLE.

...
IT'S A LONG STORY. DO YOU HAVE THE TIME, SIR?

A LITTLE MORE THAN TEN YEARS AGO...

SEI LI'S TALE

...MY WIFE WAS THREE YEARS AND SIX MONTHS PREGNANT.

OF COURSE THIS WAS ABNORMAL. NORMALLY, BABIES ARE BORN AFTER TEN MONTHS AND TEN DAYS.

MY BABY MAY BE DEAD...

BUT I SECRETLY SUSPECTED THAT THE CHILD WOULD NOT BE HUMAN.

NO NO!

A LOVELY BABY WILL BE BORN!

Y... YES!

THEN...

...SHE HAD A DREAM.

WHO?

MADAM LI...I'M SORRY, BUT YOUR CHILD IS MORTALLY MALFORMED.

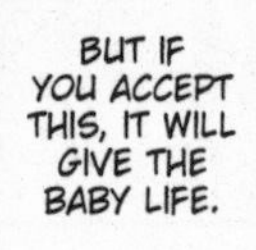
BUT IF YOU ACCEPT THIS, IT WILL GIVE THE BABY LIFE.

FLOAT

MOOM
THE PAOPE REIJU ...

NO!

I...IT'S COMING! IT'S COMING!
BOING
WH... WHAT'S COMING!
LABOR PAINS!

WH... WHAT KIND OF DREAM IS THAT?
cramp
OH?

AND THIS ODD EGGLIKE THING WAS BORN...

WH... WHAT IS THIS?!
YOUR CHILD.

UNFORTUNATELY, IT SEEMS TO BE ENCASED IN SOME SORT OF SHELL.

I CAN'T SHOW THIS MONSTROSITY TO MY DEAR WIFE!

WE'LL CUT IT AND BURY IT BEFORE INSHI SEES IT!

Y... YES!

SLASH

SHIVER

?

CRACKLE

THE CHILD ...

...WAS BORN WEARING PAOPE ...

PAOPE? WHAT A MYSTERIOUS CHILD.
I HEARD ABOUT THE DREAM AND UNDERSTOOD.
I HAD A DREAM JUST BEFORE HE WAS BORN.
A DREAM?
THAT THE MAN WHO APPEARED IN HER DREAM WAS A SENNIN, AND A PAOPE WAS EMBEDDED IN HER BELLY.
BUT I JUST COULD NOT LOVE THE CHILD, WHO I NAMED NATAKU.
THE CHILD WAS AN ARTIFICIAL HUMAN, WHO WAS CREATED USING MY WIFE...
HOW COULD YOU?!
WHAT, I CAN'T HELP IT. I DON'T LIKE HIM.
WHATEVER YOU MAY SAY, NATAKU IS OUR CHILD.
WE HAVE TO LOVE HIM AND RAISE HIM TO BE A GOOD PERSON!

BUT CONTRARY TO OUR WISHES, NATAKU GREW UP TO BE EVEN MORE DANGEROUS.
BAM BAM
NATAKU, MEAL IS READY!
IT'S GOOD.
NATAKU, TIME TO STUDY. WHAT'S 1+2?
3.
I SEE.
AND? DID SOMETHING HAPPEN AFTERWARDS?
YES...I WILL TELL YOU.
INSHI'S TALE
IT WAS THREE YEARS AGO, A HUMID DAY.
NATAKU WANTED TO GO OUT, SO WE WENT TO THE RIVER. WE WEREN'T SUPPOSED TO GO IN IT.
Isn't this fun, Nataku?
OH.

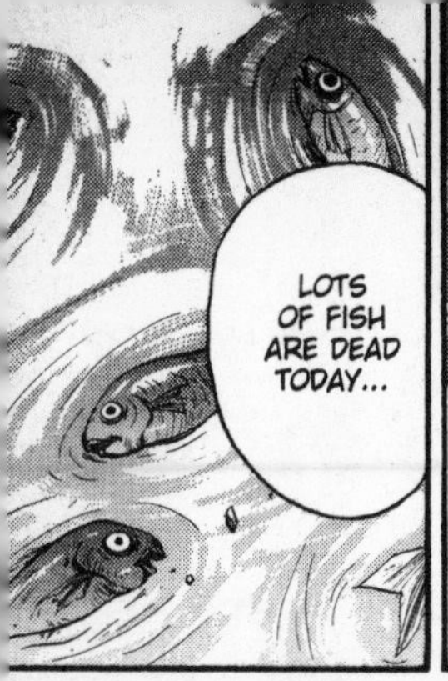
LOTS OF FISH ARE DEAD TODAY...

NATAKU... THAT CLOTH AROUND YOUR WAIST...YOUR FATHER SAID THAT IT IS A PAOPE.
HUMMMM
IT'S GLOWING AND RED.

BURBLE
WH... WHAT IS THIS?!

MOTHER ...
...PLEASE GO TO THE SHORE.
!!
GURBLE

NATAKU... YOU CALLED ME MOTHER FOR THE FIRST TIME...
BEAM
HURRY!

CRASH

WHO'S THERE ?!

WHO'S USING A PAOPE IN MY WATER?!

CRASH

OOM

THE LOINCLOTH YOU'RE WEARING IS KONTENRYO!
DID YOU KNOW THAT THE PAOPE CAUSES VIBRATION IN THE WATER?!

OH...PLEASE FORGIVE HIM. NATAKU IS JUST A CHILD...
...PLEASE, PLEASE...

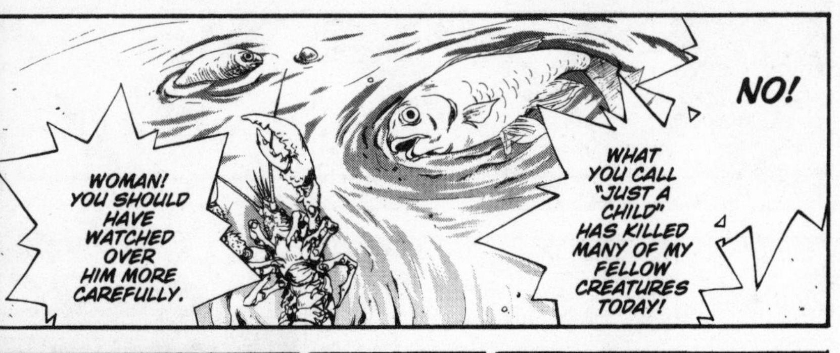

NO!
WHAT YOU CALL "JUST A CHILD" HAS KILLED MANY OF MY FELLOW CREATURES TODAY!
WOMAN! YOU SHOULD HAVE WATCHED OVER HIM MORE CAREFULLY.

I SHALL EXECUTE YOU BOTH!

NOOOO!

SSSSHHH

!!
SPLURT
BAM
NATAKU ...
CRASH
...YOU DIDN'T HAVE TO...

...
IT TRIED TO KILL YOU, MOTHER.

NATAKU... WHAT HAVE YOU DONE.
THIS IS GOHEI, THE THIRD PRINCE OF THE WATER REIJU KING.

THAT'S WHY I TOLD YOU NOT TO COME HERE!
THE REIJU WILL COME TO HAVE REVENGE ON US!

A FEW DAYS LATER ...
...AN ARMY OF THE REIJU KING'S CLAN SURROUNDED CHINTOKAN.

WHERE'S THE ONE WHO KILLED MY CHILD?!
IF HE DOESN'T COME OUT, I WILL DESTROY THIS CHECKPOINT!

OH NO...

MOTHER... PLEASE GO SOME-WHERE SAFE.
I'LL SETTLE THINGS.
NO!

FLIP
REIJU KING ...

...I WILL ACCEPT ANY PUNISH-MENT!
MY SON'S SIN IS MY SIN...

NO INSHI! I'M THE HEAD OF THE HOUSEHOLD! I'LL TAKE RESPONSI-BILITY!
NO.
GRAB
IF I DIE, THINGS WILL BE OVER.

CLUMP

MOTHER ...

...I GIVE THIS BODY BACK TO YOU.

NATAKU DIED ONCE ...

NATAKU DIED THREE YEARS AGO. BUT HE JUST APPEARED AGAIN TWO DAYS AGO...
DIED?
WAIT A MINUTE! HE'S ALIVE!
YES... HIS BODY. I WONDER WHAT'S HAPPENED.
MONSTERS COME BACK TO LIFE.
PLEASE!

BUT WELL, BECAUSE OF THAT, THE WATER REIJU'S RAGE WAS QUELLED.
NOD NOD
HUH? THAT'S THE END OF THE STORY?!

THAT DOESN'T EXPLAIN WHY NATAKU HATES HIS FATHER!
SWEAT

I...I HAVEN'T DONE ANYTHING THAT WOULD MAKE NATAKU HATE ME.
No, you must have.

READ THIS WAY

WELL, SO WE JUST HAVE TO PUT A STOP TO THIS FIGHT.
CAN YOU?
SSSSSHHHHH
UH OH... SPEAK OF THE DEVIL...

DON'T WORRY, SUPUSHAN!
I THINK WE CAN SETTLE THINGS PRETTY QUICKLY THIS TIME!
CLICK

封神演義

CHAPTER 11: TAIKOBO VS. NATAKU!!

RRROOOLLL
I-I... INSHI, LET'S GO!
TUG TUG
NATAKU!

OOO

TAIKOBO VS. NATAKU!!

Chapter 11

YOU DON'T HAVE TO READ IT, BUT SINCE THERE'S AN EXTRA PAGE:

HACK WRITING

- IN THE BOOK I READ, IT SAID THAT THE LAST KING OF THE YIN DYNASTY, KING CHU, WAS THE 30TH KING. BUT THE NOVEL SAID HE WAS THE 31ST KING. ANOTHER BOOK SAID HE WAS THE 17TH KING.
- I'VE ALSO HEARD THAT THE CAPITAL OF YIN IS NOT CHOKA BUT YIN. (THERE ARE THEORIES THAT THE YIN EMPIRE WAS CALLED SHANG AND THAT THE COUNTRY NAME YIN WAS NAMED AFTER THE CAPITAL.)
- I WANT SOMEBODY TO TELL ME THE TRUTH.
- I WISH I HAD A TIME MACHINE.

- ABOUT COLOR PAGES.
- I WANTED TO USE COMPUTER GRAPHICS USING THE MACINTOSH, BUT BECAUSE MY PRINTER BROKE, I COULDN'T.
- MY THINGS TEND TO LAST A LONG TIME, AND MY MACHINES HARDLY BREAK. BUT RECENTLY, THE SEL SATURN BROKE. I'M OVERUSING THE PLAYSTATION, SO I'M WORRIED ABOUT WHEN THAT WOULD BREAK.
- I USE COPIC FOR COLORING.
- I REALLY WANTED TO USE COLOR INKS, BUT I DON'T HAVE THE TIME. PLEASE FORGIVE ME.

END OF HACK WRITING

STOMP

NATAKU! I AM HERE TO PROTECT YOUR FATHER!

WHISTLE

WHOOOSH

IF YOU WANT TO KILL SEI LI, DEFEAT ME FIRST!

M-M-M-MASTER!
WHAT, SUPU?

UM, THIS QUARREL HAS NOTHING TO DO WITH US.
AND IT'S OBVIOUS THAT NATAKU IS MUCH STRONGER THAN YOU ARE, MASTER!
EXACTLY.

THAT'S WHY IF WE CAN MAKE HIM OUR ALLY, IT WOULD BE LIKE HAVING A THOUSAND MEN ON OUR SIDE.
SO WE NEED TO INTERVENE AND MAKE HIM OWE US ONE.

YOU HAVE A PLAN FOR WINNING, YES?
BUT...
PONDER
WHAT, YOU'RE SCARED?
A HIPPO!
LISTEN, SUPUSHAN! IF YOU'RE AFRAID AND WON'T FLY...
...YOU'RE JUST AN ORDINARY HIPPO!

HERE WE GO, MASTER!
GLARE
GO!

PLEASE ...
...TAKE CARE WITH MY SON.
I WILL ...
...DO MY BEST.
TAIKOBO !
SHO OM
HOVER

HERE!
SSSHHHH
FLICK
WHAM

SLAM
BUMP
SSSHHH
FLICK
!
WE STOPPED IT!
GRIN

HMPH.

HE REALLY WAS BORN TO FIGHT.

SSSHHH

The next panel is the left one!

BAM BAM

!
IT'S TWO THIS TIME!
OOPS!
DODGE THEM, SUPUSHAN!

HE...IS STRONG!
WOOOOO

FLICK
DON'T WORRY! I WON'T LOSE JUST LIKE THAT!

WH... WHAT AN ATTACK!
MASTER, YOU CAN'T BEAT HIM.

NATAKU!
...
WHAT HAPPENED? THEY WON'T HIT ME FROM SO FAR AWAY!

FOO

FWOO
AHHH-HHH!!!

READ
THIS
WAY

WHUP
!!

WHAT ?!
HE'S GOING TO CATCH THE PAOPE THAT HE SHOT!

FLICK

SSSHHH
OH NO!

GRIN

BEND

WOOOO
HUH?
WHAT WAS THAT?

KENKONKEN ATTACKS DIRECTLY USING COPPER RINGS.
I CAN'T STOP TWO AT THE SAME TIME, BUT I *CAN* CHANGE THE DIRECTIONS THEY FLY.

HUNH
SSSHHH

READ THIS WAY

SMASH
GAAAAH!
WAAH!

OH NO!
SEI LI AND HIS WIFE!

MOTHER!

WOOOOOOOO

SH...
...SHEESH. THIS IS DANGEROUS...

PHEW

DA
FU
BA
THERE! DAFUBA!

SPLURT
?
NATAKU!

SHOOOM

WELL, EVEN IF YOU DO, I'LL JUST USE THE DASHINBEN TO MAKE THEM FLY SOMEWHERE ELSE.

THEN YOUR DEAR MOTHER MIGHT INDEED DIE THE NEXT TIME!

THERE, YOU CAN'T USE THEM NOW!

FLASH

SOME PAOPE ARE INCOMPATIBLE. YOU CAN'T BEAT DASHINBEN WITH THE KENKONKEN!
HAHA
HA
MASTER... YOU'RE ACTING LIKE THE BAD GUY NOW...
I'm ashamed of you...

YOU...
HA HA
...WHY DO YOU INTERFERE?!

WHAT'S BETWEEN ME AND SEI LI IS NONE OF YOUR BUSINESS.
WOW! HE SPOKE!

NATAKU ...
...WHY DO YOU HATE SEI LI?
...
IT'S UNPLEASANT WATCHING A CHILD TRY TO KILL HIS OWN FATHER.
SEI LI DETESTS ME.

!

I CAN UNDER-STAND.
I WAS BORN WEARING THESE WEAPONS.
I CAN SEE WHY HE CAN'T CONSIDER ME AS HIS CHILD.

I CAUSED TROUBLE FOR MOTHER TOO.

THAT'S WHY I GAVE BACK MY BODY TO HER.

I SHOULD HAVE DIED THEN ...
...BUT THE REAL ME...
...WAS ALIVE...

MOTHER MADE A SPLENDID GRAVE FOR ME. SHE DIDN'T KNOW I WAS STILL ALIVE.
BUT A FEW YEARS LATER ...
TMP

THAT WAS ENOUGH TO MAKE ME HAPPY.
INSHI ...
...SHE MADE THIS GRAVE WITHOUT TELLING ME?!

...HE DARED TO DESTROY THE GRAVE ...
CRUMBLASH
PLINK
...AND THREW AWAY THE REIJU HE DUG OUT FROM THE GRAVE!

HOW COULD YOU ...
NOOOOO
You!
I COULDN'T HELP IT!
IF THE REIJU KING FOUND OUT ABOUT THE GRAVE, HE MIGHT HAVE GOTTEN ANGRY AGAIN...
WELL THAT'S TRUE, BUT...

READ THIS WAY

FLLOWW
THEN ...

...A SENNIN APPEARED ...

...AS I WAS LYING EXPOSED ON THE RIVERBANK.

WHO ARE YOU?!

I AM TAIITSU SHINJIN. I LIVE IN KINKODO IN MOUNT KANGEN OF THE KONGRONG MOUNTAINS.
GRIP
NATAKU... YOU ARE NOT TO DIE YET.

YOU SHALL BE BORN AGAIN AS AN INCARNATION OF THE LOTUS.

WHEN I REGAINED CONSCIOUS-NESS, LOTUS FLOWERS SURROUNDED ME.

SOMEHOW HE'S KEEPING ME ALIVE.
I DON'T KNOW WHAT HE'S DOING IT FOR.

BUT I KNOW ONE THING...
...THAT I CAN'T FORGIVE SEI LI.

I SEE.
NOD NOD
THAT'S WHY YOU WERE AFTER SEI LI...
THE BODY I RECEIVED FROM MOTHER IS GONE! MY BODY IS MADE OF LOTUS NOW...
I'M NOT RELATED TO SEI LI ANYMORE! I WON'T HESITATE!

OH ...
TAP
I'VE CHANGED MY MIND.
NATAKU, I'M WITH YOU NOW.
HURRY UP AND KILL YOUR IDIOT FATHER!
WHAAAT ?!
ooo

封神演義

Chapter 12

THE END OF NATAKU'S TALE

...

YOU CAN'T DO IT, CAN YOU?

I THOUGHT IT WAS STRANGE.
SOMEBODY LIKE YOU SHOULD BE ABLE TO KILL THIS BLOCKHEAD IN THREE SECONDS.

NO!
HE'S GOOD AT RUNNING AWAY!

NO!
YOU DON'T HATE SEI LI COMPLETELY.

READ THIS WAY

NO-NO-NO-NO-NO-NO!
NO-NO-NO-NO-NOOOOO!

No!
No!
...

NO!
I HATE SEI LI!
FLICK

MOTHER!

SMASH

MOTHER
...
MOTHER!
MOTHER!

BLOW

STEAM

THANK ME.
I PROTECTED YOUR PARENTS.

I AM ON YOUR SIDE AFTER ALL.

FLICK

NO-NO-NO!
SSS
HHH
NO-NO-NO!
WHOOM
GRIT
ENOUGH...
...NATAKU!

READ THIS WAY

SSSSHHH

HE STILL INTENDS TO FIGHT ?!
Heave ho
YOU'LL DIE IF YOU CONTINUE!

THE POWER OF A PAOPE IS WEAKENED IF YOU LOSE YOUR CONCENTRATION.
THERE'S NO WAY YOU CAN DEFEAT ME NOW!

WAIT!
GRAB

TOSS
NATAKU...

ENOUGH.

I DON'T WANT TO LOSE YOUR FATHER OR YOU...

...

FLOP

I'VE LOST.

DO WHAT YOU WANT.

I WANT TO ASK YOU ONE THING.

WHAT AM I?

WHAT AM I TO THOSE TWO?
I'M A PAOPE. MY BODY IS NOT RELATED TO THEM ANYMORE...
A HUMAN CHILD HATES HIS FATHER AT ONE POINT.
HE TRIES TO KILL HIS FATHER AND MAKE HIS MOTHER HIS OWN.
IT'S CALLED THE OEDIPUS COMPLEX.
THE MOTHER GAVE BIRTH TO THE CHILD...
...BUT THE FATHER ALWAYS WONDERS IF THE CHILD IS REALLY HIS.
HMPH
THAT'S WHAT I LEARNED IN THE SENNIN WORLD.
WHATEVER YOUR BODY IS NOW...
...I THINK YOU ARE ALWAYS FAMILY.

READ THIS WAY

...
BUZZ
BUZZ
YOU MAKE NO SENSE.
YOU'RE DENSE.

I DID UNDERSTAND THAT MOTHER SAID NOT TO KILL SEI LI.
SO I WON'T KILL HIM.

YES.
THAT'S ENOUGH, ISN'T IT?

CLAP CLAP

CLAP
CLAP

WELL DONE, TAIKOBO.
CLAP
CLAP
CLAP
YOU SETTLED THE QUARREL SO EASILY.
YOU'RE ...!
TAIITSU SHINJIN!
Taiitsu Shinjin.
One of the 12 Kongrong Elite Sennin.
He created Nataku the Reiju child.
His rank is equal to Taikobo, who is the direct disciple of Genshi Tenson.
Looking into the camera

FLAP
WELL, AS THE ONE WHO CREATED NATAKU, I WANTED TO DO SOMETHING ABOUT THIS QUARREL TOO...

HEY
...BUT I COULDN'T PLAY DIRTY TRICKS LIKE USING HIS MOTHER AS A SHIELD.

WE HAVEN'T MET FOR SO LONG. AND THAT'S THE FIRST THING YOU SAY?!
OH SORRY. IT'S BEEN 300 YEARS? LONG TIME NO SEE!
↑ He's lying.

(Sennin are immortal, so their concept of time is hazy.)

NATAKU.

YOU'RE STILL JUST A CHILD.
I'LL TAKE YOU TO THE SENNIN WORLD AND HAVE YOU TRAIN UNDER ME! WOULD YOU LIKE THAT?

WHAT?

WHO DO YOU THINK YOU ARE?
WHAT ARE YOU? TELL ME!
FLICK

IF YOU DON'T, I'LL KILL YOU!
So he's the one who created you.

WELL WELL ...
...ALL RIGHT...
HUUUUMMM

PAOPE KYURYU SHINKATO!

DAM

READ
THIS
WAY

FLIP!!

IT'S GROWING?!

BAM!!

AAH! IT CAUGHT NATAKU!
IT IS A PAOPE MADE FOR CAPTURING THINGS!

...
BY THE WAY, TAIKOBO ...
...COULD YOU HAVE SUPUSHAN TAKE ME DOWN?
SHAKE
I'M ACTUALLY TERRIFIED OF HEIGHTS.

SO I'LL TAKE RESPONSIBILITY FOR TRAINING NATAKU. PLEASE DON'T WORRY.
BANG BANG
Y...YES, SENNIN-SAMA.

BUT...
NYAAAAH
Let me out! Let me out of here!
...IT'S HEART-BREAKING. I WON'T BE ABLE TO SEE NATAKU?
Hmph

TAIKO-BO.

YOU SEEM TO BE HAVING A HARD TIME ALONE.
SO THIS MEETING MUST BE FATED.
WHEN NATAKU'S TRAINING IS OVER, HE WILL RETURN AS YOUR PARTNER.

SO BEFORE THEN, DON'T ACT IN HASTE.
BE SEEING YOU.

READ
THIS
WAY

...

I'LL GO TO THE SENNIN WORLD AND TRAIN AGAIN AS WELL.
WHAT ?!

TO TELL THE TRUTH, I RAN AWAY BECAUSE THE TRAINING WAS SO HARD.

BUT AS NATAKU'S FATHER, I CAN'T CONTINUE TO HAVE HIM BEAT ME!
I'LL GET HIM THE NEXT TIME!

SURE.

LOTS OF STRANGE FOLK IN THIS WORLD.

BUT YOU WERE REALLY STRONG, MASTER! WHAT HAPPENED?

SUPU, YOU DIDN'T NOTICE?

THERE ARE A FEW PLACES CALLED REIKETSU IN THIS WORLD. REIKI GATHER THERE.
FOR EXAMPLE, THE ROCK I WAS FISHING ON IS A REIKETSU.

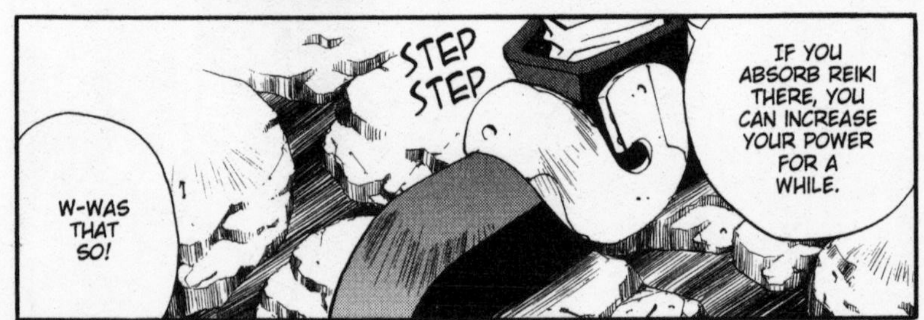
IF YOU ABSORB REIKI THERE, YOU CAN INCREASE YOUR POWER FOR A WHILE.
STEP STEP
W-WAS THAT SO!

GIGGLE. ♡

I'VE FOUND YOU, TAIKOBO. ♡

封神演義

CHAPTER 13: YOZEN!!

Choka

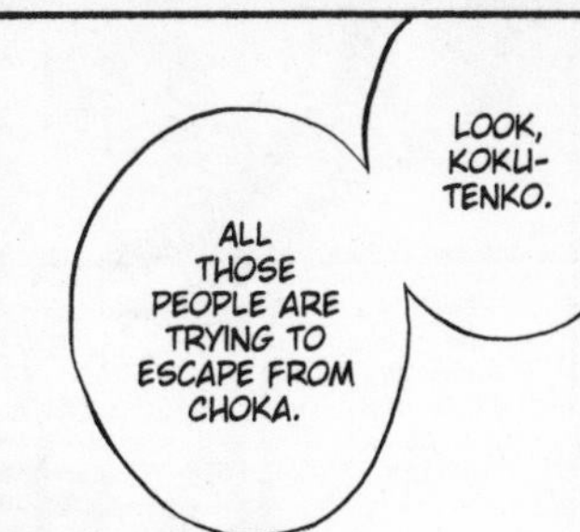

LOOK, KOKU-TENKO.
ALL THOSE PEOPLE ARE TRYING TO ESCAPE FROM CHOKA.

WELL, I DON'T BLAME THEM...
...FROM TRYING TO GET AWAY FROM DAKKI'S REIGN OF TERROR...

SHINKOHYO... DAKKI ISN'T ANYWHERE IN CHOKA.

HEH. YOU NOTICED, KOKUTENKO.
YOU'RE RIGHT. KIBI IS WITH KING CHU AS WE SPEAK.

(Kokutenko's Senrigan Vision)

BUT KIBI'S A FORMIDABLE ADVERSARY, HERSELF.
SHE'S USING BOTH THE KEISEI GENJO AND NYOI HAGOROMO SIMULTAN-EOUSLY.
L... Loli.
SHE DOES SEEM TO BE EXHAUSTED THOUGH.
THEN WHERE'S THE REAL DAKKI?

...
SHE'S PROBABLY *THERE.*
HUH?
WHAT'RE YOU TALKING ABOUT?
THE COLOSSAL TIDE THAT'S STIRRING BEHIND DAKKI...
LET'S CALL *IT* THE "HISTORY'S GUIDEPOST" FOR NOW.

Chapter 13
YOZEN!!

TMP
TMP

TMP
TMP

...

SUPU, LISTEN TO ME! DON'T TURN AROUND.
HUH? WHAT IS IT?
TMP
TMP
SOME-ONE'S FOLLOW-ING US.
WHAAAT?!
I TOLD YOU NOT TO TURN AROUND!

...
AND ...
SNIFF
...HAVEN'T YOU SMELT THIS BEFORE?
SMELL?
SMELL?

M...M... MASTER, THIS IS DAKK...
PANIC
SHHH! CALM DOWN, CALM DOWN!

LISTEN.
WE COUNT TO THREE THEN TURN AROUND. ALL RIGHT?

READ
THIS
WAY

CLENCH
ONE...

GRIP
...TWO
...

...THREE
!
BAWHAM

WH...
WHAAT
?!
SNORT

TH...
THIS
IS!

BAM
BAM
BAM
DAKKI!
WA
WHAM
OOOH, IT'S BEEN SO LONG. ♡

HUNH?

FOOSH
NOOOO!
FLAP FLAP

SUPU...
I...I CAN'T STAND...

GIGGLE ♡
SPARKLE
SHINE

I FOUND YOU, TAIKOBO. ♡
I KNEW YOU DIDN'T DIE! ♡

WH...WHY IS DAKKI HERE?!

TO KILL YOU, SILLY...
...SUPU-SHAN. ♡

HMM?
I DO FEEL SORRY FOR YOU...

...BUT WITH THIS NEW PAOPE, SANSENTO ...
...I'LL TURN YOU INTO SASHIMI. ♡

SASHIMI?
Oh no!

STOP IT, DAKKI!
SLAM

FLUTTER

ARE YOU GOING TO FIGHT ME?
YOU'RE NO MATCH FOR ME...
...TAIKO-BO. ♡

WELL WELL, YOU SURPRISED ME!
YOU APPEARED PRETTY SUDDENLY AND STRANGELY.

IT'S NOTHING STRANGE. ♡
I KNEW THAT YOU WERE ALIVE.
I WAS GOING TO LEAVE YOU ALONE...
...BUT EVEN SMALL WOUNDS...
...CAN GET INFECTED. ♡

THERE. ♡

SKKRAAAAPE

WHISTLE
WELL THEN, TAIKOBO!
ATTACK ME WITH ALL YOUR STRENGTH! ♡
HAHAHAHAA

I DIDN'T THINK I'D END UP HAVING TO FIGHT DAKKI.

I HAVE NO CHOICE.

I'M COMING, DAKKI!

CLENCH

FWISH

GLARE

SLAM

BAM
GIGGLE ♥

BLINK
POP

READ THIS WAY

?
SHOOM
SOMETHING'S WRONG.

DAKKI'S NOT THE TYPE TO LEAD AN ATTACK HERSELF...
SHE LETS HER MINIONS DO THE WORK. SHE'S A RULER.

BUT SHE'S ALL ALONE...

IS IT SOME SORT OF TRAP AGAIN?
TWITCH

WELL TAIKOBO ... ♡
SHF
I'LL CHARM YOU WITH MY DEADLY ALLURE! ♡
SHF

EH ...
TWITCH

AHA-
HAHA.
SHIVER
HA!
I CAN'T TAKE IT ANYMORE! YOU'RE A FAKE, AND YOU'RE MAKING ME LAUGH!
!

A...A FAKE?
YES!

YOU LOOK EXACTLY LIKE DAKKI, BUT YOU DON'T HAVE HER DOWN AT ALL.
YOU'RE SO AWKWARD IT'S EMBARRAS-SING TO WATCH.
HAH!

PLUS, THE REAL DAKKI CALLS SUPU "SUPU"...
...NOT "SUPU-SHAN"!

!!
I EVEN KNOW WHO YOU ARE.
I'VE HEARD ABOUT THE AMAZING DOSHI IN THE SENNIN WORLD WHO HAS PERFECTED ***TRANSFORMATION JUTSU.***
(Mount Kongrong)
WHAT WAS HIS NAME...
...YONIN... NO... IT'S...

...YOZEN!

OH NO!
GRP
YOU SAID MY NAME!

CONGRATU-
LATIONS
ON SEEING
THROUGH MY
DISGUISE.

I'M YOZEN,
DISCIPLE OF
GYOKUTEI SHINJIN
OF KINKADO
IN MOUNT
GYOKUSEN OF
THE KONGRONG
MOUNTAINS.

FWUMP

!!

WOW, HE'S BEAUTIFUL. AMAZING!

HE LOOKS MORE LIKE A HERO THAN YOU!

Shut up.

THINK ABOUT IT, SUPU.

DOINK

HE WAS PRETENDING TO BE DAKKI.

HE WAS SAYING "I'LL CHARM YOU ♡"!

POSE ♡

Heh

PLEASE DON'T...

AND?
WHY'D YOU DO THAT?
WE MEET FOR THE FIRST TIME, AND THIS IS THE WAY YOU GREET ME?

...

GENSHI TENSON-SAMA GAVE ME AN ORDER.

I'M TO ASSIST ON THE HOSHIN PROJECT.
!!

WELL IN THAT CASE!
FLOAT
WELCOME!

IF YOU'RE AS MUCH A TALENTED GENIUS AS THEY SAY, THEN I CAN FINALLY RELAX AND LET YOU DO ALL THE WORK!

FWIP

HOW-EVER...

...I AGREED ON ONE CONDITION.

ONE CONDI-TION?

THAT I BE ALLOWED TO TEST WHETHER TAIKOBO IS WORTHY OF WORKING FOR...

...AND IF HE ISN'T, I SHALL EXECUTE THE HOSHIN PROJECT AND DEFEAT DAKKI!

封神演義

Chapter 14

YOZEN'S TEST

A few months ago, in the Sennin World
SHWOO
SHWOO
HELLO, HAKUTSURU DOJI! I HEARD THAT GENSHI TENSON-SAMA HAS CALLED FOR ME...
WILL YOU TELL HIM THAT I'M HERE?
FLAP
HELLO YOZEN. WE HAVE BEEN WAITING FOR YOU!
FLAP
IT LOOKS AS IF YOU WILL RECEIVE AN IMPORTANT ORDER.
AN ORDER ...

READ THIS WAY

Gyoku-kyokyu

DOSHI YOZEN IS HERE!

AH, YOZEN!

DOSHI.

YOU ALREADY HOLD THE SENNIN LICENSE. CALL YOURSELF A SENNIN.

I CANNOT DO THAT.

THERE IS AN APPRENTICE SYSTEM FOR SENNIN ...
...THEREFORE IF I CALL MYSELF A SENNIN, I NEED TO TAKE DISCIPLES.
I PREFER TO USE MY TIME TO POLISH MY SKILLS, RATHER THAN TRAIN DISCIPLES.

YOU'RE A GENIUS, THE ONLY ONE IN THE SENNIN WORLD WHO CAN PERFORM MIRACLES USING YOUR "JUTSU" WITHOUT EVEN USING PAOPE.
AND STILL YOU WISH TO TRAIN HARDER...
SO, THEN.
TODAY I CALLED YOU FOR SOMETHING ELSE.
SOME-THING ELSE?

I HAVE A DIRECT DISCIPLE, THE DOSHI TAIKOBO.
I WOULD LIKE YOU TO ASSIST HIM ON A VERY IMPORTANT PROJECT THAT HE WILL EXECUTE.

IS THAT ...
...THE HOSHIN PROJECT ?
YES... YOU KNEW ABOUT THIS?
...
GENSHI TENSON-SAMA, EXCUSE ME FOR INTERRUPTING. WOULDN'T IT BE DISCOURTEOUS TO HAVE HIM WORK UNDER TAIKOBO?
FLAP
FLAP

READ
THIS
WAY

HAKUTSURU, DO YOU BELIEVE THAT YOZEN IS MORE CAPABLE THAN TAIKOBO?
EVERYBODY KNOWS THAT! THIS IS A SHAME FOR YOZEN!

STOP IT, HAKUT-SURU.
RISE
Ah!
Yozen ...
I ACCEPT THIS PATH!

I HAVE ONE CONDITION THOUGH.
DOINK
CONDI-TION?

I DON'T KNOW HOW CAPABLE THIS DOSHI TAIKOBO IS.

THEREFORE I WOULD LIKE TO TEST HIS ABILITIES...
ZZZ
...TO SEE WHETHER HE IS WORTH WORKING FOR...

A TEST?

I WILL HAVE YOU TAKE THREE TESTS.

THE FIRST TEST IS ALREADY OVER.
WHEN YOU FACED DAKKI, YOUR BIGGEST ENEMY, YOU STAYED CALM.
YOU PASSED.
GRR
AND THE TEST CONTINUES?

OF COURSE ...

SNAP

...IT WILL!

GROOOWR

WHAT'RE YOU?!
BARK
STRUGGLE
LET ME GO!
LET ME GO!
WRIGGLE
THAT DOG...IS NOT A REIJU.
EXACTLY! HE'S KOTENKEN, MY PAOPE.
I'm a dog.
HIS ABILITIES TO KILL AND WOUND ARE SUPERIOR.
GO KOTENKEN! BITE SUPUSHAN!
BUN
GLARE
BOW!

GYAAAA!

TAIKOBO ...

(Doesn't look scary at all...)

SUPU-SHAN!

GRIN

...YOU NEVER FIGHT USING YOUR TRUE POWERS.

HEY SUPU!

Go for it! Yeah!

BITE HIM BACK! DO IT!

Yozen

I...I CAN'T...

I'M NOT MADE FOR FIGHTING...

SOB SNIFFLE

Grp

ARE YOU GOING TO CONTINUE PLAYING DUMB?

TAIKOBO!

SLAM

SLAM

MASTER!

DRIP

DRIP

WHY DIDN'T YOU DODGE IT?!

YOZEN.
IT DOESN'T MATTER WHO WINS THIS FIGHT.

...
HMPH

I LIKE THAT, SUSU.
YOU DON'T HESITATE EVEN IF YOU MAY HURT YOURSELF.

READ THIS WAY

YOU PASS THE SECOND TEST AS WELL.

WHAT SHALL I DO NOW? I HADN'T DECIDED WHAT TO DO FOR THE THIRD TEST.
SKUF
IS THERE ANY WAY TO TRULY TEST YOUR POWERS?
YOU ASSUMED I'D FAIL ONE OF THOSE TESTS.
UH-HUH.

SHEESH... YOU MAY BE A GENIUS, BUT YOU'RE TOO FRANK AND NASTY.
HUH?

THE ARM THAT GOT BITTEN DOESN'T HURT AT ALL.
I HAD KOTENKEN GO EASY ON YOU.

HEEEY HEEEY!

SOME-ONE'S COMING.
HEEEY!
I KNEW IT!
IT WAS YOU, DOSHI!

READ THIS WAY

WHY'RE YOU HERE, FIREWOOD SELLER?
DID YOU MOVE OUT OF CHOKA?

PLEASE LOOK AT THAT.
BECAUSE OF THE HEAVY TAXES, THE PEOPLE DON'T HAVE ENOUGH TO EAT...
...AND MORE AND MORE PEOPLE ARE DYING. MOSTLY CHILDREN AND OLD FOLKS.
WE CAN'T TAKE IT ANYMORE!
CLEN CH
...
CHOKA IS FINISHED.

TRUDGE...

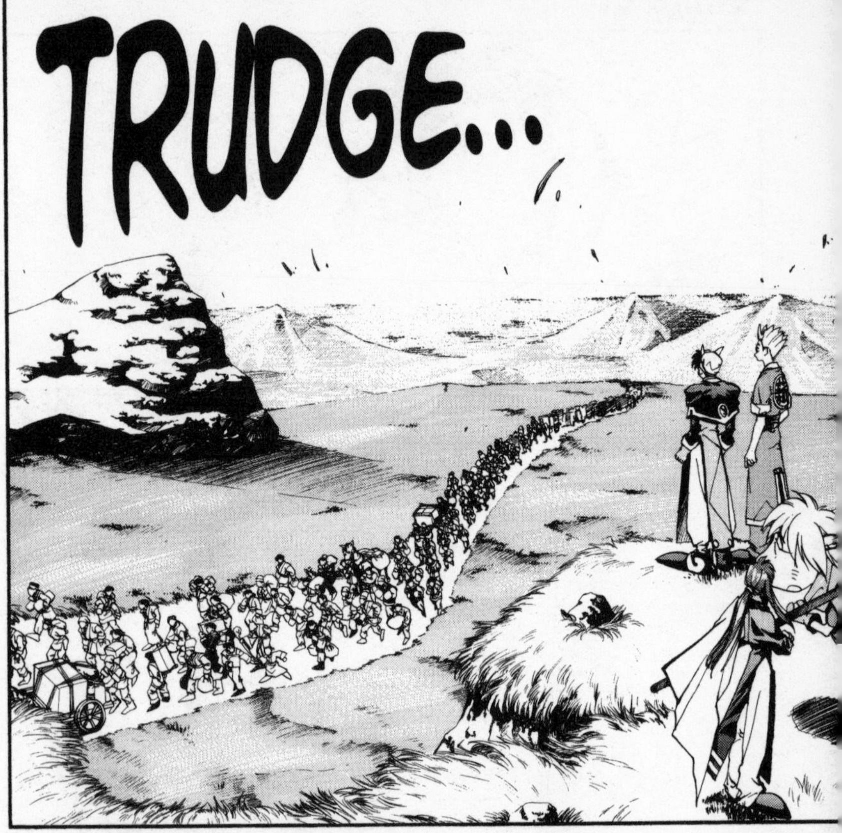

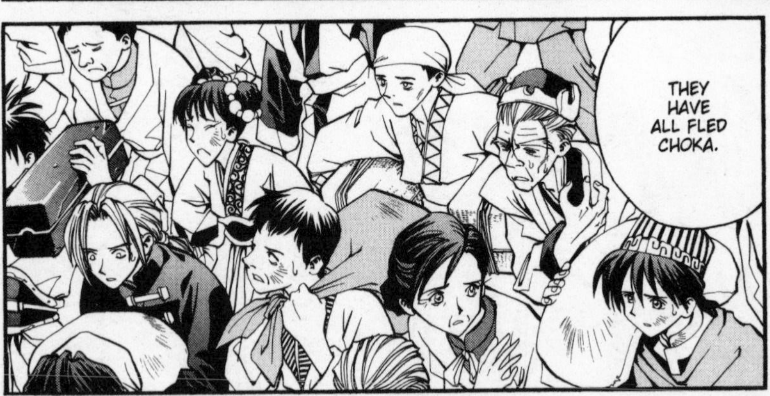
THEY HAVE ALL FLED CHOKA.

READ
THIS
WAY

WE PLAN TO GO TO SEIKI.
Seiki
The Metropolitan Area
WE HEAR THE WESTERN REGION STILL HAS WORK AND GOODS.

BUT CAN YOU LEAVE THIS AREA SAFELY?

WELL ...

...TO LEAVE, WE HAVE TO PASS THROUGH THAT RINTOKAN ...
...BUT ACCORDING TO THE PEOPLE WHO ARE IN FRONT, THEY WON'T LET US PASS.

OF COURSE NOT. DAKKI WILL NOT ALLOW THAT TO HAPPEN.
SHE'S NO DOUBT GIVEN ORDERS NOT TO OPEN THE GATE.

DOSHI-SAMA, PLEASE DO SOMETHING WITH YOUR FORTUNE-TELLING!
MY FORTUNE-TELLING CAN'T DO EVERYTHING.

I KNOW!

TAIKOBO! PLEASE HELP THESE POOR SOULS REACH THE WEST SAFELY!
THIS SHALL BE YOUR THIRD TEST!

SPARK

THIS IS INDEED A QUANDARY.
ALL THESE PEOPLE.

SIMMER

IF YOU CAN SOLVE THIS PROBLEM, I WILL RECOGNIZE YOU AS MY BETTER!
FLAME

WHO DO YOU THINK YOU ARE?!

WHAT MAKES YOU ACT SO SUPER-IOR?!

HUH

WHA...

A TEST?! YES, YOU'RE INDEED A GENIUS!

TMP

THEN SHOULDN'T MR. GENIUS RESCUE THE REFUGEES?

TMP

HALT

BUT I DON'T WANT TO BACK DOWN AND REGRET IT.

HMPH... YOZEN! I WILL MAKE YOU SUFFER A LITTLE!

封神演義

Rintokan

HMPH... HOW LONG DO THOSE REFUGEES INTEND TO STAY THERE?
WHY DON'T I KILL THEM ALL!

SHAWOO
HUH?

THAT'S ...

CHAPTER 15: THE END OF THE TEST

Chapter 15

THE END OF THE TEST

CRMBL

I'VE GOT A QUESTION ...
WHO'S THE HEAD OF THIS CHECKPOINT ?
I...I'M HO CHO, THE SOHEI.
SENNIN-SAMA, WHAT DO YOU WANT?
Sohei = short for Soheikan, the rank of the military in command soldiers at a fort or similar army station.
GRIN

YOU HAVE ALL THOSE REFUGEES HANGING OUT THERE.
HOW ABOUT I GET RID OF THEM?

FOOOO

I WILL MAKE YOU SUFFER A LITTLE!

HEY YOU! THE DOSHI WENT TO THE CHECKPOINT.
WHAT'S GOING ON?!

NO...
IS HE GOING TO PLAY A DIRTY TRICK AGAIN?

THE DOSHI SAID SOMETHING ABOUT "LETTING YOU TAKE CARE OF THE REFUGEES"!
GASP
THAT MEANS YOU'RE A DOSHI TOO! THIS WAY THEN!
"... What did I do to deserve this?

STARE

OH, DOSHI-SAMA!
Noooo !
PLEASE LET US PASS THAT CHECKPOINT SOMEHOW!

GRRR!
FLINCH

...

NO MATTER WHERE TAIKOBO WENT OFF TO...
...HE WON'T ABANDON THESE PEOPLE!
WHAT HAPPENED AT THE TAIBON MUST HAVE BEEN A TRAUMATIC EXPERIENCE FOR HIM...

SOMETHING LIKE THAT CANNOT HAPPEN AGAIN...SUSU UNDERSTANDS THAT TOO!
HUH?

DOSHI-SAMA?

I HAD BEEN TAILING HIM, AND SAW WHAT HAPPENED THERE.
BUT I COULDN'T INTERVENE.
NO...THERE WAS NOTHING I COULD DO IN THAT SITUATION.

CLICK
NO WAY!

DOSHI-SAMA, DID YOU CONVINCE THE BIGWIG AT THE CHECKPOINT TO LET US THROUGH?
WOW!
SNORT

!!

DOSHI-SAMA, WHAT'RE YOU...

YOZEN IS ON YOUR SIDE.
Hmph.
THEN I'LL GUARD THE CHECKPOINT.

Y...
AAAAH
...YOU TRAITOR!

GLARE

WAHAHAHAHA!
SHABOOM
AHHHH!

OH NO! DO WE HAVE TO GO BACK TO CHOKA?!
BUT EVEN IF WE GO BACK, THE EMPRESS IS STILL THERE!
...

READ
THIS
WAY

TAIKOBO... YOU DON'T EVEN DESERVE TO BE TESTED!
YOU HARASS ME, AND EVEN INVOLVE THE PEOPLE IN THIS!

GENSHI TENSON-SAMA! YOU'VE MADE A MISTAKE!
BAM

FWUMP
TRANS-FORM!

!

WELL THAT WAS AMAZING, DOSHI!
THE STUPID MASSES ARE ALL RUNNING AWAY!

NO... LOOK AT THAT, HO CHO!
OOO
?!

SHINE SHINE

AS MENTIONED BEFORE, THE BUSEIO IS RESPONSIBLE FOR ALL MILITARY AFFAIRS.

ALL CHECKPOINTS IN THE COUNTRY ARE UNDER THE BUSEIO'S COMMAND.

B-B-...

...BUSEIO ?!

HO CHO ...

...WHAT IS GOING ON HERE?

H... HUH?

WHY WON'T YOU LET THE PEOPLE PASS THE CHECK-POINT?!
DON'T YOU UNDERSTAND WHAT I'M ASKING?!
WINCE
B...BUT BUSEIO ...
FLINCH

IT'S AN ORDER FROM THE EMPRESS! HERE!
VE
This is an order. ♡ Absolutely do not let those who fled Choka pass Rintokan. ♡ Dakki
SHO
THIS IS THE WRITTEN DIRECTIVE!

THAT ORDER HAS BEEN CHANGED.
LET THE PEOPLE PASS!
YES!
STOMP
DON'T LET HIM FOOL YOU!

THAT BUSEIO IS A FAKE!
HE'S REALLY A DOSHI FROM THE SENNIN WORLD IN DISGUISE! DON'T BE FOOLED!

WHAT?

A...A FAKE?

SIZZLE

ALL RIGHT, HO CHO. YOU DECIDE!

YOU DECIDE WHO'S TELLING THE TRUTH.

...

Grrrr

GRRR

CAPTURE THAT SHADY DOSHI!
AAH!
.....
KNOCK

I THANK YOU, BUSEIO!
I WAS ABOUT TO BE DUPED BY THIS STUPID DOSHI AND END UP COMMITTING A TERRIBLE ACT!
Master...

SOME-THING'S WRONG...

SUPUSHAN'S ALWAYS THE FIRST ONE TO LECTURE SUSU...

MASTER...

IF YOU KEEP DOING THINGS LIKE THIS, PEOPLE WILL HATE YOU EVEN IF YOU MEAN WELL.

WHY DIDN'T HE SAY ANYTHING?

HA!

IF YOU JUST LOOK AT THE RESULT, THE REFUGEES DID PASS THE TEST...AND NO ONE BUT SUSU GOT HURT...

SHUFFLE

COULD IT BE...

D...NO, BUSEIO, THANK YOU SO MUCH!

DASH

READ
THIS
WAY

YOU, HOW COULD YOU!
KICK
KICK
NO, PLEASE STOP!

HUH?

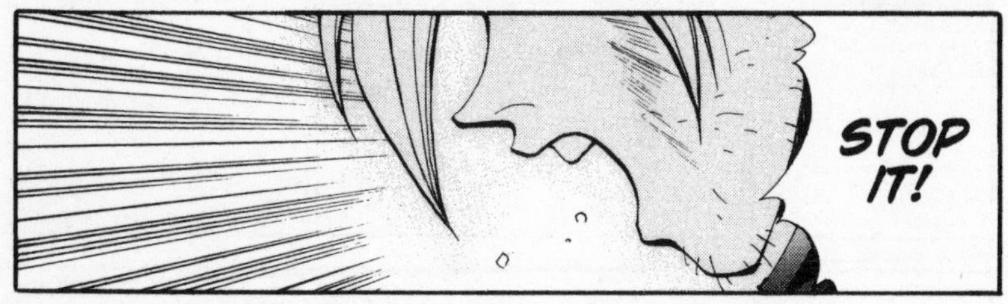
STOP IT!

TAIKOBO ...

...YOU'RE REALLY...
GRIN

YOZEN IS INDEED A GENIUS.
HE CAN MAKE PAOPE PERFECTLY. HIS JUTSU IS PERFECT TOO.
BUT HE'S A GENIUS ONLY IN THE SENNIN WORLD.

THEN YOU MEAN THAT IN THE HUMAN WORLD HE'S NOT?
...

HAKUTSURU, I ASK YOU.
WHOM WOULD YOU PREFER TO WORK UNDER, YOZEN OR TAIKOBO?

!
YOU NOW UNDERSTAND? THE ONE WHO EXECUTES THE HOSHIN PROJECT MUST BE A LEADER.
HE DOES NOT NEED TO BE A GENIUS.
HE MUST BE ABLE TO MAKE PEOPLE WORK TOGETHER, HAVE COMPASSION FOR THE MASSES... AND MAKE EVERYONE WANT TO ASSIST HIM.

READ THIS WAY

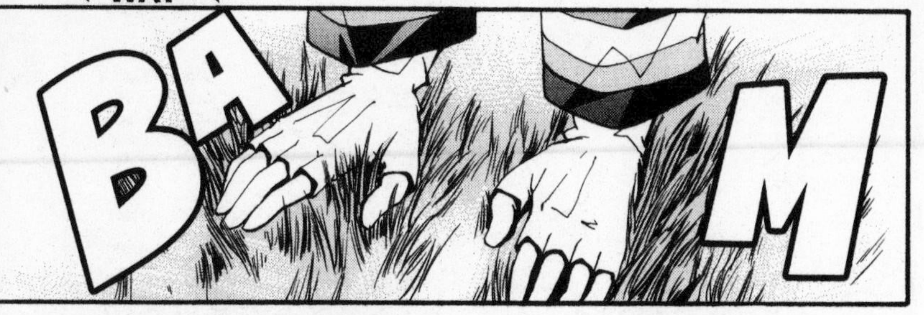
BAM

I APOLOGIZE, TAIKOBO!
I'M ASHAMED OF MYSELF.
YOU EVEN USED ME TO SAVE THOSE PEOPLE.
THAT WAS AMAZING!
WHAT ABOUT IT, SUPU. I EVEN DUPED YOZEN THE GENIUS!
HaHa!
THAT!
IS THE PROBLEM!
DOINK
YOU'RE A DOSHI, BUT I DO THINK YOUR BEST TALENT MAY LIE IN SUCH SIMPLE DECEPTIONS...
?

I WAS REALLY CONFIDENT THAT I COULD TRANSFORM INTO DAKKI.
BUT YOU SAW THROUGH IT SO QUICKLY... I NEED TO WORK ON MY ACTING. ♡
FWUMP

I HONESTLY DON'T THINK I AM CONFIDENT ENOUGH TO BE WORKING WITH TAIKOBO RIGHT NOW. ♡
BLINK BLINK
I MUST RETURN TO THE SENNIN WORLD AND PRACTICE MY ACTING. ♡

DASH
ALL RIGHT, GOODBYE TAIKOBO. UNTIL WE MEET AGAIN! ♡

WHAT?! YOU'RE NOT GOING TO ASSIST ME RIGHT NOW?!
TA DA
BECAAAAAUSE I'M A PERFECTIONIST! ♡

HOOO HOHO-HOHO!
HE KIND OF SEEMED TO LIKE THAT A LITTLE TOO MUCH, RIGHT?

READ THIS WAY

...
FWUMP

SUSU...THE SKY OF CHOKA IS FILLED WITH THE AIR OF DISTURBANCE.
RUMBLE
CRACK
PLEASE HURRY TO THE WEST BEFORE IT'S TOO LATE.

I SHALL COME BACK WHEN IT'S TIME TO SERVE YOU.

Choka

HMM ...

OH!

SISTER DAKKI! ☆

HUNH
HEY, WHAT'RE YOU DOING? WHAT? WHAT? WHAT? ☆
HUNH
Sigh...
I CAN'T THINK OF ANYTHING ...

I WONDER IF THERE'S ANYTHING MORE FUN THAN THE HORAKU OR THE TAIBON. ♡
KIBI WILL THINK WITH YOU. ☆
BUT THERE'S SOMETHING ELSE TOO ...
SIGH

READ THIS WAY

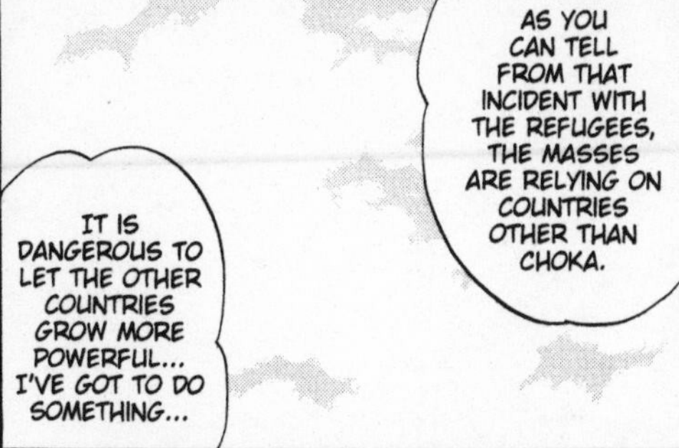
AS YOU CAN TELL FROM THAT INCIDENT WITH THE REFUGEES, THE MASSES ARE RELYING ON COUNTRIES OTHER THAN CHOKA.
IT IS DANGEROUS TO LET THE OTHER COUNTRIES GROW MORE POWERFUL... I'VE GOT TO DO SOMETHING...

BOO-HOO. THAT'S NOT LIKE YOU, SISTER. ☆
LET'S DRINK, EAT SOMETHING AND RELAX. ☆

DRINK ...
POP
EAT SOMETHING ?!

FAN
OK! ♡
I JUST THOUGHT OF SOMETHING, KIBI. ♡

SHUCHI NIKURIN.

SHINE

SPARKLE

LET'S GO WITH THAT. ♡

("Shuchi Nikurin" refers to sumptuous feasts. The word comes from a banquet that King Chu apparently held, where there was a pond of liquor and meat on trees. The kanji for Shuchi Nikurin literally mean "liquor-pond-meat-woods.")

封神演義

NATAKU AND YOZEN...
TAIKOBO MANAGED TO CREATE CONNECTIONS WITH THESE POWERFUL TWO.

CHAPTER 16: DAKKI'S BANQUET

HE'S NOW HEADING OUT WEST. NO ONE QUITE KNOWS WHY.

ON THE OTHER HAND, DAKKI...

SMASH

KSSHH KSSHH KSSHH KSH

DAKKI...

...WHAT'RE YOU BUILDING THIS TIME?

HUF

Chapter 16

DAKKI'S BANQUET

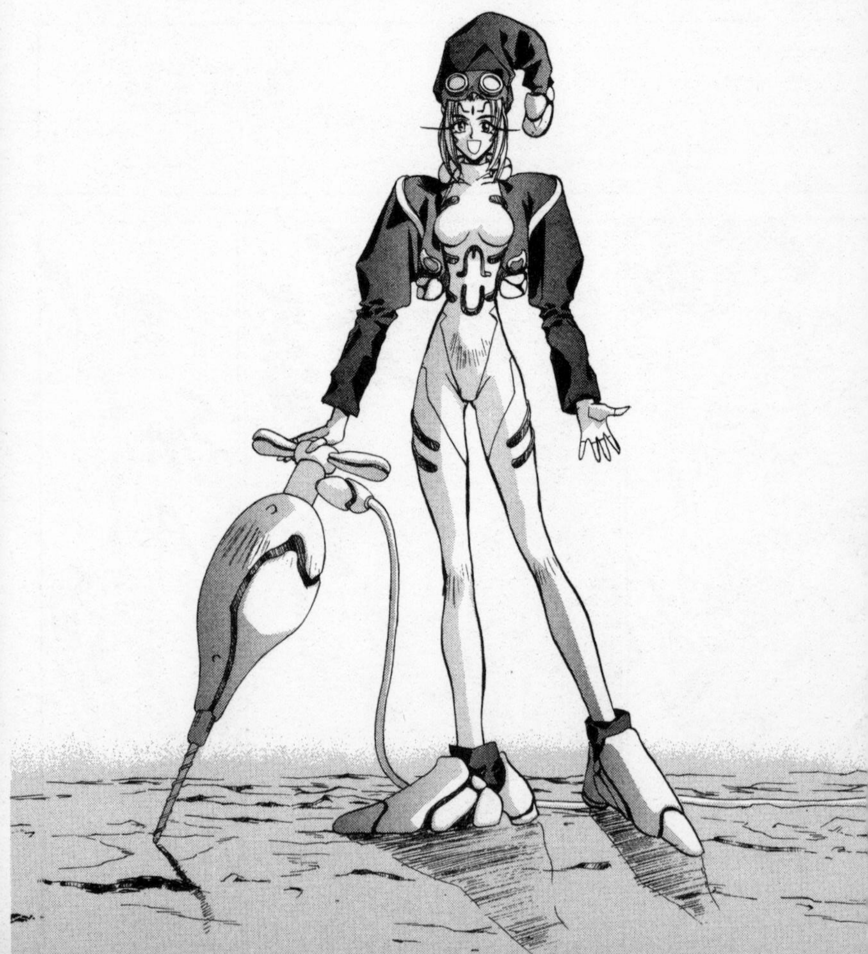
SHUCHI NIKURIN! ♡

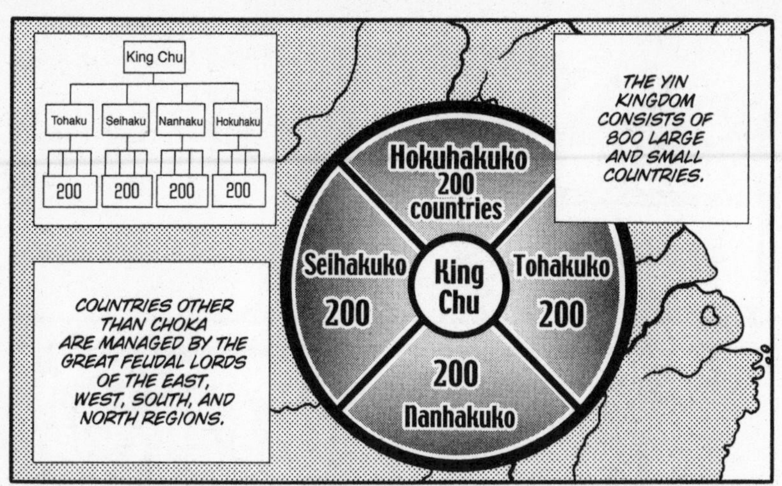
THE YIN KINGDOM CONSISTS OF 800 LARGE AND SMALL COUNTRIES.
Hokuhakuko 200 countries
Tohakuko 200
King Chu
Seihakuko 200
200 Nanhakuko
King Chu
Tohaku
Seihaku
Nanhaku
Hokuhaku
200
200
200
200
COUNTRIES OTHER THAN CHOKA ARE MANAGED BY THE GREAT FEUDAL LORDS OF THE EAST, WEST, SOUTH, AND NORTH REGIONS.

Tohakuko Kanso Kyo

Seihakuko Sho Ki

Hokuhakuko Koko Su

Nanhakuko Su Gaku

IN PARTICULAR, THE REPUTATION OF SHO KI, THE GREAT FEUDAL LORD OF THE WEST REGION, IS SPREADING ALL OVER THE LAND.
Seiki Castle

Invitation ♡
I am Dakki. ♡ The young love of King Chu's life. ♡
I plan to hold a wonderful banquet. All the Four Great Feudal Lords, pleeeease come. ♡
Sincerely

FATHER, WHAT IS THIS?
AN INVITATION TO A WONDERFUL BANQUET.

THIS IS AN EXCELLENT OPPOR-TUNITY.

SHIIIFF
THERE ARE RUMORS THAT KING CHU HAS GONE OUT OF HIS MIND, AND THAT CHOKA IS IN A TERRIBLE STATE.
I WILL GO TO CHOKA TO SEE WHETHER THAT IS TRUE.

I AM WORRIED.

HAKUYUKO. AS MY ELDEST SON, YOU TAKE CARE OF POLITICAL AFFAIRS WHILE I'M GONE.
EVEN IF SOMETHING HAPPENS TO ME, DO NOT LEAVE SEIKI. I SHALL RETURN.

Thus the Four Great Feudal Lords assemble in Choka.

HMM.

THE FOR-BIDDEN PALACE ...
IT IS INDEED A MAGNIFICENT AND BEAUTIFUL PALACE...

BUT...

YES.
THE PEOPLE OF CHOKA DON'T SEEM VERY WELL-OFF.

THAT'S ALL RIGHT.
THE MASSES ARE MEANT TO BE EXPLOITED BY THEIR RULERS.
HMPH.

KOKO SU! HOW CAN YOU ...
LUNGE
STOP IT!

WE FOUR ARE THE CHIEFS OF THE 800 FEUDAL LORDS OF THE LAND!
CALM DOWN!

CLIMP

HEY HEY! ☆

FWAP FWAP

YOU GUYS MUST BE THE FOUR GREAT FEUDAL LORDS!

KIBI WILL SHOW YOU TO THE BANQUET VENUE! ☆

OH, THIS *IS* A LOVELY YOUNG LADY!

THEN PLEASE SHOW US THE WAY!

THIS BANQUET IS GOING TO BE REALLY FUN! ☆

THERE'S SO MUCH LIQUOR, EVEN A WHALE CAN'T DRINK IT ALL! THERE'S FOOD TOO! ☆

HAHAHA! THEN WE'LL GET DOWN TO WORK!

HURRAH

YAY, CHUGALUGG♡ CHUGALUGG♡ CHUGALUGG♡
(WORDS AND MUSIC BY DAKKI)♡
HURRAH

GASP

OH! ♡

WELCOME, THE FOUR GREAT FEUDAL LORDS! ♡

WELCOME TO THE SHUCHI NIKURIN PARTY! ♡

SHUCHI NIKURIN?

WOW, AMAZING!
SPLOSH
THE WATER IN THIS POND IS ALL LIQUOR!

WHAT A WASTE... SO THIS IS SHUCHI, THE POND OF LIQUOR...

THEN "NIKURIN," THE WOODS OF MEAT ARE...
WAAAH!
!

A TIGER ?!

GRROWRR

SPLI
SH

DRIP
DRIP

YOUR MAJESTY!
WHAT IS THIS?!

GUNGH GAH URK
DROOL
HE'S ASKING YOU "WHAT ARE YOU ANGRY ABOUT?" ♡

SNORT

WHERE DID ALL THIS LIQUOR COME FROM?
GRRRROWWR
WHAT IS THAT TIGER EATING?!

WE COLLECTED EVERY DROP OF LIQUOR FROM THE MASSES OF CHOKA. ♡
AND WE'RE USING, WELL, I GUESS ABOUT 500 SLAVES AND CRIMINALS AS FEED FOR THE TIGER! ♡

KING CHU! YOU MUST STOP THIS!
YOU WILL NOT ONLY LOSE THE TRUST OF THE PEOPLE, BUT YOUR SUBJECTS WILL FORSAKE YOU TOO!
NO...

I WORKED NIGHT AFTER NIGHT FOR THIS PARTY... OH!
FAINT
D...DAKKI! ARE YOU ALL RIGHT?!

GLARE

HOW COULD YOU...

KANSO KYO! SU GAKU!

DO YOU DARE SAY THAT YOU ARE NOT PLEASED WITH THE EMPRESS'S BANQUET?!

BUSEIO.

YOU'RE
...

DO YOU KNOW?
THERE'S SOMETHING AMAZING GOING ON IN THIS PALACE.

WHAT
?

DRIP
DRIP

D...DAKKI. YOU DIDN'T HAVE TO KILL THEM ...
THE COUNTRY OF YIN IS STABLE BECAUSE THE FOUR GREAT FEUDAL LORDS GOVERN THE 800 COUNTRIES.
NOW YOU'VE KILLED THEM, THE PEOPLE OF THE EAST AND SOUTH MIGHT REBEL ...

NO!
FLASH
AS LONG AS KING CHU RULES, YIN WILL NOT PERISH! ♡
I...IS THAT SO?
YES, OF COURSE! ♡
HOW SMART YOU ARE, DAKKI!
...

HIS MAJESTY IS BEING MANIPULATED BY THIS EXQUISITE BEAUTY!
SHE... DAKKI IS NOT HUMAN... HER BEAUTY AND CRUELTY... SHE IS A MONSTER!
↑(Boat)
ARE YOU ENJOYING THE SHUCHI NIKURIN?
AND WHAT ABOUT YOU TWO?
URK
OF COURSE!
FLATTER FLATTER
I'M AMAZED. A BEAUTIFUL LADY THINKS UP OF SOMETHING THAT AN ORDINARY PERSON CANNOT!
FLATTER
OH KOKO SU... ♡
AND YOU, SHO KI?
I...
...I...

SHOOOO
WE FELL IN HER TRAP.
DAKKI PLANNED TO KILL US FROM THE VERY BEGINNING...
...TO WEAKEN THE FOUR GREAT FEUDAL LORDS...
THAT FIENDISH WOMAN!

BUT I MUST ADMONISH HIS MAJESTY.
EVEN IF I DIE BECAUSE OF IT, THAT IS MY LOYALTY TO MY LORD...

YOUR MAJESTY ...

A BANQUET LIKE THIS IS OUTRAGEOUS.

READ
THIS
WAY

SHO
KI!

THEN YOU TOO ...
STEP
YOUR MAJESTY! EMPRESS!

!

WELL WELL, AND LORD SHO KI TOO! IT'S BEEN FAR TOO LONG!
TA
DA
BUSEIO!

OH! ♡
YOU CAME TO ENJOY THE SHUCHI NIKURIN?!

CERTAINLY ...
I'M RATHER OFFENDED YOU DIDN'T INVITE ME, EMPRESS.

WELL, LORD SHO KI! LET'S ENJOY THE BANQUET OF LIQUOR AND BLOOD!

B...BUT BUSEIO ...

OH! ♡

NO NO, BUSEIO! ♡

WIGGLE

SHO KI SAID HE DIDN'T LIKE THIS PARTY.
AND NOW I HAVE TO KILL HIM.
BECAUSE IF I FORGIVE SHO KI, WHAT ABOUT THE POOR TWO WHO DIED? ♡

PLEASE DO NOT!
SHO KI IS TRULY A LOYAL SUBJECT!
IF YOU EXECUTE HIM, YOU WILL LEAVE A HUGE BLOT ON YIN'S HISTORY!
YES ...
SHO KI HAS SUPPORTED ME IN MANY WAYS...

YES... BUT I CANNOT LET HIM GO FREE. ♡

I WILL NOT EXECUTE HIM. INSTEAD, I WILL HAVE HIM IMPRISONED FOR LIFE! ♡
PHEW

NOW HANG THOSE TWO CORPSES FROM THE TREE. ♡
THE BANQUET WILL BE IN FULL SWING NOW! ♡

DAKKI-SAMA...
...SHOULD YOU HAVE LET HIM LIVE?

HMPH

I WAS GOING TO KEEP SHO KI ALONE ALIVE.
I STILL NEED HIM FOR SOMETHING...

KANSO AND SU DIED...
DRIP
DRIP
...AND KOKO SU IS ACTING LIKE THAT...
FLATTER
Here's something to drink.
Ooh thank you! ♡
THIS IS REGRETTABLE...

THUS DAKKI'S PLOT SUCCEEDS.
SEIHAKUKO SHO KI IS IMPRISONED IN THE COUNTRY OF YURI NEAR CHOKA FOR SEVEN YEARS.

THIS SHO KI BECOMES "KING BUN" OF ZHOU, THE ERA THAT SUCCEEDS YIN.

SHINKOHYO, WHY DID YOU TELL BUSEIO ABOUT THE SHUCHI NIKURIN?

BY MEETING BUSEIO, SHO KI WAS ABLE TO MAKE A CONNECTION WITH TAIKOBO.

TAIKOBO IS HEADING WEST TO SEE SHO KI.

THE CONNECTION BETWEEN TAIKOBO, SHO KI, AND BUSEIO BECOMES IMPORTANT LATER.

THEY BECOME ALLIES, AND WAGE A GREAT WAR AGAINST DAKKI...

...WON'T THAT BE EXCITING, KOKUTENKO ?!

CHARACTE ENCYCLOPEDIA!!

WE REVEAL THE HIDDEN PAST OF THE MAIN CHARACTERS!

Taikobo Ryobo (Shiga Kyo)

DATA: Doshi. Age 72. Main character of this story.

He's been through a lot! What was the young Taikobo like?!

◆Taikobo is 72 years old now. He started training as Doshi in Kongrong Mountains when he was 12. What was he doing after he lost his peaceful life as the son of the head of the Qiang clan, and before he started training...? After Taikobo lost everything, he avoided Yin, and lived a wandering life, taking care of cattle.

◀ Great split-second timing!

▲ Great acting when he's in a tight spot! His heart is in it!

Shinkohyo

DATA: Doshi. Age 1000 and ?. Taikobo's rival.

The real schemer is Shinkohyo? What is he thinking?!

◆He corners Taikobo, then helps him out of a desperate situation. Shinkohyo acts whimsically. What is his standing in the Sennin World? He's been given Raikoben, the strongest paope, and he moves freely between the Human World and the Sennin World. Therefore although he is a Doshi, he is treated like a Sennin, and is important enough that even Genshi Tenson acknowledges him.

▲ He's furious that Taikobo said he has no taste! His blank look is a distinguishing feature!!

◀ Great combination with Kokutenko, who's a droll comical act!!

SU U EXPLAINS TH SEC TS OF PAOPE!

SHIJU HAGOROMO		KARYUHYO		RAIKOBEN		DASHINBEN	
Flying & Nerve Disruptor	Okijin	Chemical Reaction	Shinto	Chemical Reaction	Shinkohyo	Attack	Taikobo
The powder of poisonous moths that was discharged from Okijin's Shiju Hagoromo spread far out, so Master had a hard time.		Master says it's a weak paope, but Chinto's Karyuhyo is a powerful paope that can manipulate flames at will.		Raikoben is called the strongest paope. It is a frightening paope that causes lightning and thunder, and reduces the opponent to ashes. I don't want to remember it.		Master's Dashinben is a paope that manipulates wind to hurt his opponent. He can wield it in close combat as well as from far away.	

HOSHIN ENGI SECRET

HOSHIN ENGI, IN WHICH TAIKOBO STARS IN ANCIENT CHINA!

MEET THE CHARACTERS!!

Dakki So

DATA: Empress. Age 1000 and ?. Taikobo's greatest enemy.

She's actually a sweet girl who loves her father?!

▲ Dakki in her fox mode. These eyes are really scary!!

▲ Her sweat after she's worked sparkles because she's Dakki...?!

◆ Dakki manipulates King Chu, and is the main cause of the devastation of Yin. The current Dakki is actually a Sennyo who has borrowed her body and taken over her soul. The real Dakki is the daughter of the Soshi clan. Her beauty became famous, and the womanizer King Chu asked her to enter the harem. If she refused, the clan would be punished. She grievingly accepted, thinking of her father, but unfortunately...!

King Chu

DATA: 30th King of the Yin Dynasty. Age unknown.

He can easily win against cows and tigers! He has Herculean strength?!

◆ Manipulated by Dakki, King Chu does not show a glimpse of his former wise self anymore, but he was apparently very competent before he married Dakki. He was smart, and his physical abilities far surpassed that of an ordinary human. The Imperial Court was full of capable staff. The Lords of 800 countries vowed loyalty, and the world was supposed to be in peace.

I SPENT HUNDREDS OF YEARS PERFECTING THIS TEMPTATION JUTSU. ♡
WITH THIS JUTSU, I'VE OBTAINED THE HIGHEST STATUS. ♡

▲ King Chu is dallying. He can't help it...

▼ King Chu as a lifeless shell. His mind's gone!

SPECIAL VEHICLES

Supushan

I can boast about my flying speed. I can't tell you about the ball I'm holding yet.

Kokutenko

I don't like him, because he's got glaring eyes. There are rumors that he's ferocious enough to eat Yokai...

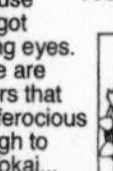

KENKONKEN

Attack | **Nataku**

There aren't many paope that can destroy as much as Nataku's Kenkonken can. Will Master be all right?

NYOI HAGOROMO

Transformation | **Kokibi**

Kokibi's paope is different from her two sisters' paope. It is a transformation paope. She can even dupe King Chu with her transformation.

KEISEI GENJO

Nerve Disruptor | **Dakki**

Keisei Genjo is a Hagoromo that radiates the perfume of temptation. I caused trouble for Master because of this perfume.

This article was published in Issue 39, in 1996 of *Weekly Shonen Jump*.

THE SHEEP PRECIPICE, WHERE IS IT NOW?

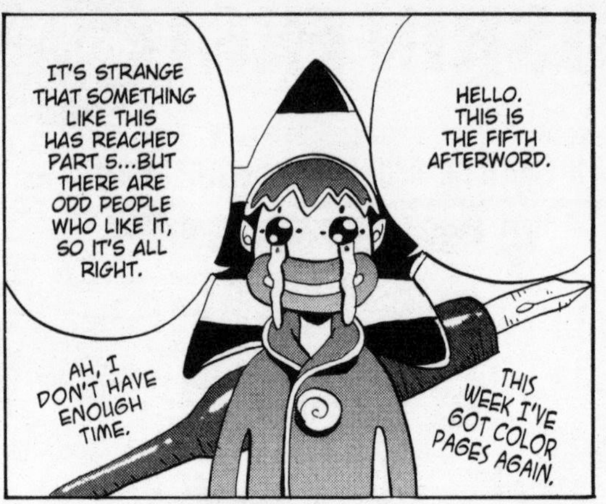
HELLO. THIS IS THE FIFTH AFTERWORD.
THIS WEEK I'VE GOT COLOR PAGES AGAIN.
IT'S STRANGE THAT SOMETHING LIKE THIS HAS REACHED PART 5...BUT THERE ARE ODD PEOPLE WHO LIKE IT, SO IT'S ALL RIGHT.
AH, I DON'T HAVE ENOUGH TIME.

THIS TIME WE TAKE QUESTIONS FROM THE READERS.
LETTER
ZIP CODE 123456 INDIA

HMM... WHAT WHAT? WHAT'S THE BALL THAT SUPUSHAN'S HOLDING?
THIS WAS THE NO. 1 QUESTION.

THEN LET'S ASK HIM.
POP
THIS IS THE REIJI SUPUSHAN!

THIS IS A MYSTERIOUS BALL THAT HAS BEEN PASSED DOWN FOR GENERATIONS.

BLINK
YES, SO EVEN HE DOESN'T KNOW.
END OF QUESTIONS !

BY THE WAY, THERE ARE PEOPLE WHO DO HOSHIN ENGI COSPLAY.

I RECEIVED PHOTOS.

FUJISAKI HAS NEVER GONE TO THE COMIKET FOR EXAMPLE, SO I DON'T KNOW ABOUT THESE THINGS TOO WELL.
THE PEOPLE I SAW IN THE PHOTOS
SHINKOHYO
DAKKI-CHAN
APPARENTLY, THERE ARE DIFFERENT KINDS OF EVENTS. MAYBE I'LL GO SOMEDAY.
POSE

OH, AND MR. SHIMA. WHAT HAPPENED TO THE ONE-WEEK TRIP TO CHINA TO GATHER MATERIALS FOR THE MANGA?
WHAT HAPPENED... YOU HAVE NO TIME. YOU CAN'T TAKE A WEEK OFF.

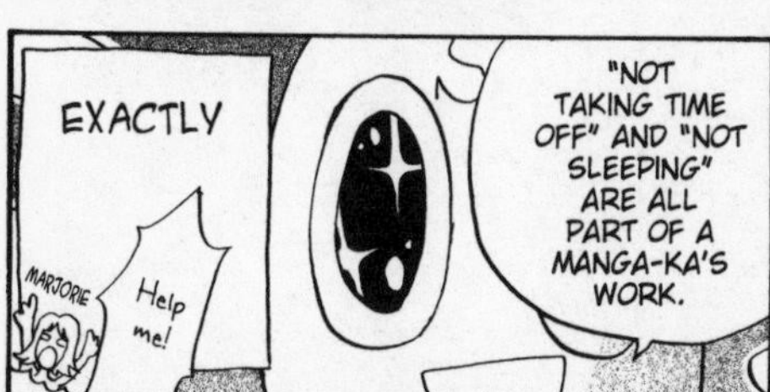

"NOT TAKING TIME OFF" AND "NOT SLEEPING" ARE ALL PART OF A MANGA-KA'S WORK.
EXACTLY
Help me!
MARJORIE

Something's happening without the manga-ka knowing.

Hoshin Engi: The Rank File!

You'll find as you read *Hoshin Engi* that there are titles and ranks that you are probably unfamiliar with. While it may seem confusing, there is an order to the madness that is pulled from ancient Chinese mythology, Japanese culture, other manga, and, of course, the incredible mind of *Hoshin Engi* creator Ryu Fujisaki.

This glossary has been compiled by VIZ Media as a guide for terms used in *Hoshin Engi*. It did not appear in the Japanese edition. Where we think it will help, we give you a hint in the margin on the page the name appears.

Japanese	Title	Job Description
武成王	Buseio	Chief commanding officer
大諸侯	Daishoko	Great feudal lord
軍師	Gunshi	Military tactician
北伯侯	Hokuhakuko	Lord of the north region
上大夫	Jotaifu	Court ranking similar to "Lord"
南伯侯	Nanhakuko	Lord of the south region
宰相	Saisho	Premier
西伯侯	Seihakuko	Lord of the west region
総兵官	Soheikan	A military rank, in command of soldiers at places like forts where armies are stationed
太師	Taishi	The king's advisor/tutor
東伯侯	Tohakuko	Lord of the east region

Hoshin Engi: The Immortal File

Also, you'll probably find the hierarchy of the Sennin, Sendo and Doshi somewhat complicated. Here, we spell it out the easiest way possible!

Japanese	Title	Description
道士	Doshi	Someone training to become Sennin
仙道	Sendo	Used to describe both Sennin and Doshi
仙人	Sennin	Those who have mastered the way. Once you "go Sennin" you are forever changed.
妖孽	Yogetsu	A Yosei who can transform into a human
妖怪仙人	Yokai Sennin	A Sennin whose original form is not human
妖精	Yosei	An animal or object exposed to moonlight and sunlight for more than 1000 years

Hoshin Engi: The Magical File

Paope (宝貝) are powerful magical items used by Sennin and Doshi. Sometimes they look like regular objects, like a veil or hat. These are just a few of the magical items, both paope and otherwise, that you'll encounter in *Hoshin Engi!*

Japanese	Magic	Description
打神鞭	Dashinben	Known as the God-Striking Whip. This is Taikobo's paope. Click! WHAM!
風火輪	Fukarin	Wind Fire Wheels that allow you to fly!
五火七禽扇	Goka Shichikin'o	A fan made from the feathers of seven types of raptors that can discharge five types of flame.
火竜鏢	Karyuhyo	The Flame Boomerang
傾世元禳	Keisei Genjo	A veil that emits the "perfume of Temptation," protection against enemy attacks.
乾坤圏	Kenkonken	Shoots circles of copper at your target
金霞帽	Kinkabo	Keeps you sane! A golden hat that protects a psychological attacks.
混天綾	Kontenryo	The heaven silk can vibrate liquid quickly.
哮天犬	Kotenken	The Howling Dog can fly and be used as an attack paope.
九竜神火罩	Kyuryu Shinkato	The Nine Dragon Basket of Fire is used to capture the enemy.
如意羽衣	Nyoi Hagoromo	Transformation veil
雷公鞭	Raikoben	The Thunder Whip
霊獣 / 霊珠	Reiju	There are different types of reiju, which basically means a "magical entity." For example, Taikobo's flying pal, Supu, is a reiju in the form of a flying beast. 霊獣 is kanji for spirit/soul + beast. Another type of reiju is the Soul Sphere, which can create a human paope out of an unborn child. 霊珠 is the kanji for spirit/soul + sphere.
三尖刀	Sansento	A three-pointed sword that can create shock wav
紫綬羽衣	Shiju Hagoromo	Disguised as a purple veil, this paope allows the user to fly and emits a deadly poison.

Coming Next Volume:
Precogs

New enemies! And Taikobo gets more than he bargained for when he takes over the protection of two young princes prophesized to be part of a much larger master plan. As he unearths more of the truth of the Hoshin Project, Taikobo finds that he may never be able to trust anyone ever again.

AVAILABLE OCTOBER 2007!

Read Any Good Books Lately?

Hoshin Engi is based on *Fengshen Yanji (The Creation of the Gods,* written in the 1500s by Xu Zhonglin) one of China's four classic fantastical novels of adventure, magic and mystery. The other three are *Saiyuki* (*Journey to the West* by Cheng'en Wu, late 1500s), *Sangokushi Engi* (*Romance of the Three Kingdoms* by Guanzhong Luo), and *Shui Hu Zhuan* (*Outlaws of the Marsh,* by Shi Nai'an, mid-1500s).

Want to read these books? You can! They're all still in print, more than 500 years later!

These books are North American in-print editions only.

CAN YUGI FIGHT HIS WAY TO THE TOP OF THE DUEL MONSTERS TOURNAMENT...AND EARN THE TITLE OF DUELIST KING?
SJ
MANGA ON SALE NOW!
Yu-Gi-Oh! Duelist
SHONEN JUMP GRAPHIC NOVEL
Kazuki Takahashi
volume 1
$7.95
Yu-Gi-Oh!™ • DUELIST •
SHONEN JUMP
On sale at:
www.shonenjump.com
Also available at your local
RATED T
VIZ media

SUBSCRIBE TODAY & BECOME A MEMBER OF THE SHONEN JUMP SUBSCRIBER CLUB...
You'll get:
*Access to Exclusive Online Content!
*50% Savings Off the Newsstand Price!
*Exclusive Premiums!
All this available ONLY to Subscribers!
SHONEN JUMP
THE WORLD'S MOST POPULAR MANGA
FILL OUT THE SUBSCRIPTION CARD ON THE OTHER SIDE, OR SUBSCRIBE ONLINE AT:
www.shonenjump.com